Origins of AI in Gaming

Epris E. Ezekiel

Copyright 2024© Epris E. Ezekiel
All rights reserved. This book is copyrighted and no part of it may be reproduced, distributed, or transmitted in any form or by any means, including photocopying, recording, or other electronic or mechanical methods, without the prior written permission of the publisher, except in the case of brief quotations embodied in critical reviews and certain other non-commercial uses permitted by copyright law.
Printed in the United States of America
Copyright 2024© Epris E. Ezekiel

Contents

- Chapter 1 6
- What Is AI in Gaming? 6
- Chapter 2 13
- AI's Role in Improving Gameplay 13
- Chapter 3 19
- What Are the Pros and Cons of AI in Video Games? .. 19
- Chapter 4 25
- A Technological Symphony: AI and Gaming Platforms. 25
- Chapter 5 29
- AI in game development 29
- Chapter 6 34
- What is the future of AI in the gaming industry? 34
- Conclusion 43

The Evolution

In this article, we look at the use of artificial intelligence in gaming, from early instances like Pac-Man to sophisticated algorithms in more contemporary games like "Middle Earth Shadow of War." The article explores AI's importance in creating immersive experiences and how it has evolved to influence game design with features such as customizable NPCs, generative content creation, and increased image quality. It also discusses the potential future of AI in gaming, including autonomous game development and upgrading non-player characters with human-like intelligence and emotions.

The 1950s and 1960s: The Pioneers of Gaming AI

- ✓ The first occurrences of AI in games date back to the 1950s. One of the earliest instances is Arthur Samuel's checker's software.

- ✓ In the 1960s, "Spacewar!" appeared as one of the first video games, incorporating primitive AI-controlled opponents.

1970s and 1980s: The Arcade and 8-Bit Era.

- ✓ Arcade games such as "Pong" (1972) and "Space Invaders" (1978) used simple AI algorithms to control the movement of on-screen objects and adversaries.

- ✓ In the 1980s, prominent home consoles such as the Nintendo Entertainment System (NES) offered increasingly advanced artificial intelligence. Games like "The Legend of Zelda" (1986) and "Metroid" (1986) introduced a more dynamic gameplay experience.

Other Key Milestones and Statistics

- ✓ Pac-Man's ghosts were among the first AI-controlled characters with unique patterns and personalities, significantly improving the gameplay experience.

- ✓ By 1985, AI-controlled characters in games like "Super Mario Bros." began to react to player actions, such as chasing or running, introducing a new level of engagement and difficulty.

Thanks to advances in artificial intelligence (AI) technology, video games have changed dramatically in recent years. AI is transforming the gaming business, allowing for more dynamic gameplay experiences and lifelike interactions. We'll look at the technical implementation of AI in video games, see instances of AI-driven features and characters, and consider the impact of AI on the gaming scene.

The Turning Point

As gaming took on new dimensions, AI advanced dramatically, progressing from simple algorithms to incredible feats of technological prowess. Let's look at some key moments in the evolution of AI in gaming:

AI Integration in 3D Games

- ✓ The 1990s saw a shift toward 3D gaming, with systems like the PlayStation and Nintendo 64 opening the way for more advanced AI.

- ✓ Games with intelligent enemy characters, pathfinding, and situational awareness included "Super Mario 64" (1996) and "Half-Life" (1998).

- ✓ The late 1990s and early 2000s also saw the introduction of complex AI frameworks like as F.E.A.R.'s Goal-Oriented Action Planning (GOAP) system, which enabled NPCs to make more complicated decisions based on available actions and global conditions.

The Quantum Leap: Breakthroughs and Cutting-Edge AI Technology

- ✓ AI technology has advanced dramatically over the last few decades, including machine learning, neural networks, and natural language processing.

- ✓ Games like "The Elder Scrolls V: Skyrim" (2011) and "The Witcher 3: Wild Hunt" (2015) demonstrated improved AI behavior, providing players with a more immersive experience.

- ✓ Procedural content generation gained traction, resulting in games such as "Minecraft" (2009) and "No Man's Sky" (2016), which featured nearly endless, AI-generated worlds.

Notable Statistics and Innovations

- ✓ As of 2023, OpenAI's GPT-4, a cutting-edge natural language processing AI, has 175 billion parameters, demonstrating the possibility for AI-generated conversations and tales in games.

- ✓ According to Newzoo, the worldwide video game business will be worth $159.3 billion in 2020, with artificial intelligence playing a critical role in improving gameplay experiences and driving industry growth.

The advancement of AI in gaming has been nothing short of remarkable. As we continue to push the limits of what is possible, AI technologies will surely play an increasing role in developing the next generation of gaming experiences.

Chapter 1

What Is AI in Gaming?

Artificial intelligence in gaming refers to responsive and adaptive video game experiences. These AI-powered interactive experiences are typically generated by non-player characters, or NPCs, that behave intelligently or creatively as if they were directed by a human game player. AI is the engine that governs NPC behavior in the game world. While AI in some form has long been present in video games, it is now regarded as a thriving new frontier in game development and play. AI games gradually delegate control of the game experience to the player, whose actions contribute to the game experience.

In game design, AI procedural generation, also known as procedural storytelling, refers to game data that is generated algorithmically rather than by a developer.

This is how artificial intelligence (AI) can improve gaming immersion. But what does this mean in practice?

You've undoubtedly played Pacman before. It is one of the most well-known early examples of artificial intelligence. Four different-colored ghosts follow Pacman as he attempts to collect every dot on the screen.

They do not follow Pacman, and they appear to attempt to ambush him while he is playing. How did they do it? Every ghost is programmed to respond to Pacman's location.

One ghost will roam, while the other will fiercely pursue Pacman. Another ghost will pursue Pacman in the same direction until Pacman catches up to it.

The final ghost will follow Pacman when he is far away but will travel to a certain area on the map when Pacman is nearby.

These four behaviors give the ghosts the appearance of having a will, even though they are playing a 1980 game. They feel alive.

That is why artificial intelligence in video games serves its purpose.

What is the significance of AI?
Almost every game makes use of artificial intelligence in some fashion. Without artificial intelligence, games would struggle to provide an immersive experience.

The AI's purpose is to immerse gamers as deeply as possible. This is accomplished by making the game's characters appear lifelike even though the setting is fantasy.

As AI advances, the options for how it interacts with players' experiences alter.

Consider "Middle Earth: Shadow of War" and its nemesis system. The open-world adventure game by Monolith Productions features a variety of opponent orcs.

They have various personalities, attributes, and applications. Any orc you encounter in the game can join you, betray you, or spy for you.

The nemesis system enhances the most memorable moments of gameplay.

For example, beating an orc chieftain may result in the creation of an opponent who will pursue you into the future and remind you of your previous actions.

This feature seeks to provide players with a new way to engage with the game's NPCs. It seems personal when an orc captain assassinates your favorite ally, Orcish.

The game grows more intense when the difficult adversary you've spent hours defeating reappears at the worst conceivable time.

This game is adapted to the player's actions and features procedurally generated characters. Every gamer will have a different experience.

Despite all of this technology, the program continues to follow pre-programmed instructions from the game producers.

A comparable game might have AI that makes use of modern technology. It could feature orcs who not only appear to scheme or befriend the player but also plot and experience emotions for it.
It would be a game in which the player's actions impact the outcome.

Understanding AI in video games.
AI in video games refers to the usage of computer-controlled entities with intelligent behavior and decision-making abilities. These entities can range from non-player characters (NPCs) and enemy characters to intricate game systems that respond to player actions and preferences. The technical implementation of AI in video games consists of the following components:

Decision-making algorithms
AI characters make judgments based on a variety of criteria, including player actions, ambient conditions, and game objectives. Decision-making algorithms, such as finite state machines (FSMs) and utility-based systems, assist AI characters in selecting appropriate actions and behaviors.

Machine learning
Some video games use machine learning techniques to develop AI models that can learn and adapt to player behavior over time. Reinforcement learning methods, neural networks, and genetic algorithms can be utilized to develop AI agents that improve with experience.

Behavior Trees
Behavior trees are hierarchical structures that represent the decision-making process of AI-controlled characters. They comprise nodes that represent actions, conditions, and priorities, allowing developers to create sophisticated behaviors and replies.

Path Finding Algorithms
Pathfinding techniques help AI characters navigate gaming areas efficiently. A* search, Dijkstra's algorithm, and navigation meshes are popular methods for calculating the best pathways while avoiding obstacles and dangers.

The Effects of AI on the Gaming Landscape
AI integration in video games has had a significant impact on the gaming scene, influencing player experiences, game design, and industry trends. AI-powered elements and characters enhance immersion, increase replayability, and open up new gameplay options. Furthermore, AI technology

allows developers to create more dynamic and responsive gaming environments in which player actions have significant repercussions and interactions with AI characters feel real and engaging.

Examples of video games featuring AI.
F.E.A. R
F.E.A.R. (First Encounter Assault Recon) is known for its advanced enemy AI, which uses tactics including flanking, taking cover, and coordinating attacks to outmaneuver players. The AI adjusts to the player's strategies, making each confrontation surprising and fierce.

StarCraft II
StarCraft II has advanced AI opponents who engage players in real-time tactical battles. The AI uses complicated decision-making algorithms to manage resources, develop units, and carry out strategic operations, posing a stiff challenge to players of all skill levels.

Half-Life 2.
Half-Life 2 introduced the concept of "Director AI," a dynamic AI system that modifies game difficulty and pacing in response to player performance. To maintain tension and challenge players, the Director AI dynamically creates opponents, modifies ambient circumstances, and initiates programmed events.

The Elder Scrolls V
Skyrim includes a dynamic AI engine that controls the behavior of NPCs and creatures in the game world. NPCs demonstrate realistic behaviors like as daily routines, social interactions, and combat strategies, resulting in a rich and engaging gameplay experience.

Chapter 2

AI's Role in Improving Gameplay

Artificial intelligence has played a critical part in the evolution of gaming, resulting in more engaging, immersive, and dynamic experiences. Let's look at some significant implementations of AI in gaming and see how they've improved gameplay:

Valiant Companions: Smarter NPCs

Lifelike NPCs:
AI has allowed for the development of more realistic and intelligent non-player characters (NPCs) who exhibit human-like behaviors, emotions, and interactions. AI-driven characters in games such as "Red Dead Redemption 2" (2018) and "The Last of Us Part II" (2020) have distinct personalities and react realistically to the player's actions, providing complexity to the virtual world. These intelligent NPCs are constructed utilizing techniques like Finite State Machines, Behavior Trees, and Utility AI, which enable them to respond intelligently and dynamically to player actions and world events.

Adaptive and dynamic gaming environments:
AI systems can automatically generate tailored enemy encounters based on the player's behavior.

One example is the Nemesis System in "Middle-earth: Shadow of Mordor" (2014). This system monitors how players interact with opponent characters and alters the game world appropriately, resulting in unique rivalries, alliances, and narratives tailored to each player's specific experience.

Enchanted Worlds: Procedural Content Generation

Unlimited gaming worlds and replayability: AI-powered procedural content generation allows for the construction of essentially limitless game environments, resulting in various and distinct gameplay experiences. Titles such as "Minecraft" (2009) and "Elite Dangerous" (2014) demonstrate the enormous possibilities of procedurally produced content. These games use algorithms to generate terrain, structures, and resources at random, making each playtime unique and entertaining.

Minecraft's procedurally created worlds stand out.

Personalized gaming experiences.
AI algorithms can dynamically adjust gameplay factors such as game complexity, level design, and even stories to accommodate individual player preferences. Games like "Left 4 Dead" (2008) and "Resident Evil 4" (2005) use AI-driven algorithms to monitor players' performance and adapt gameplay based on their skill levels, resulting in a more fun and personalized experience.

The Master Craftsmen's Advanced Game Design Tools

AI-powered level design and game balance:
AI-powered design tools can help developers create complex, well-balanced levels, making the development process more efficient. For example, the puzzle game "Baba Is You" (2019) uses an AI-assisted tool known as the "Constraint Solver" to help develop its levels. The technology guarantees that each level follows specific rules and limits, resulting in tough and rewarding gameplay experiences.

Streamlined development processes:
AI can speed up prototype and asset generation, saving development time, resource utilization, and overall expenses. Promethean AI, a startup launched in 2018, provides an AI-powered platform that helps artists create gaming backgrounds with minimal user input. By analyzing reference images and understanding the artist's vision, the AI can

generate complex 3D scenes automatically, freeing up developers to focus on other aspects of the game.

AI Techniques for Gameplay Enhancement	Description	Impact on the gameplay experience.
AI-powered Animation and Physics	AI models create realistic animations and physics simulations for persons and objects.	More vivid and immersive gaming makes in-game exchanges feel more natural.
AI-generated quests and storylines.	AI algorithms generate dynamic and adaptive in-game objectives and stories based on player decisions.	Improved replayability and varied game experiences for each participant.

Dynamic Difficulty Adjustment (DDA).	AI modifies game difficulty in real time based on players' performance and playstyle.	Personalized challenges for each player, improving interest and enjoyment
AI-powered Pathfinding and Navigation	AI systems let NPCs identify optimal paths and navigate difficult surroundings.	Smoother and more realistic NPC movement enhances immersion and game interactions.

As artificial intelligence expands its influence on the gaming industry, we can expect to see even more innovative applications that enhance gameplay and immerse players in captivating, interactive worlds. The future of gaming is a thrilling adventure that is being shaped, in large part, by the heroes and sidekicks of AI.

Chapter 3

What Are the Pros and Cons of AI in Video Games?

What are the advantages and disadvantages of AI's evolving status and new technologies? These are just a few of the many advantages and disadvantages to consider as we enter a new era of gaming.

AI: Pros

As AI advances, we should expect shorter development cycles since AI can do more of the workload. The capacity to procedurally build characters and places will become more sophisticated.

There will be no random NPCs strolling around with only one or two statuses. They will have a variety of options to improve the experience.

It's also amazing to observe how NPCs can experience actual emotions. This will significantly alter the way players interact with them.

You can either care strongly about the residents of the town you are defending, or you can despise the terrible adversary who always appears to be one step ahead until you beat them.

AI has numerous potentials that are always expanding, but it also presents some challenges.

Cons of AI:
As artificial intelligence becomes more advanced; game developers lose more control. This could mean foregoing the well-crafted environments and levels we've grown to expect in favor of something simpler but more robotic.
This may be comparable to how Unity users can determine whether a game was made with stock components. It could have an impact on the whole experience.

This also implies that if the AI programming fails, we may see more confused games. In Aliens: Colonial Marines, for example, the AI adversaries acted in strange ways, destroying the immersion.

Will we be able to eliminate or manage this problem? It is tough to determine. There is also the prospect that AI will be able to undertake more game programming on its own, potentially affecting the careers of many of the top game designers now working in the business.

The benefits of AI in gaming
AI has made important contributions to the gaming industry, bringing several benefits that have altered how we play and enjoy games.

Collaboration between humans and artificial

intelligence leads to increased creativity.

Exploring new ideas and stretching game boundaries:
AI can help developers experiment with new concepts, unusual gaming mechanisms, and inventive storytelling strategies. As artificial intelligence evolves, it will continue to offer up new possibilities for creativity, pushing developers to create breakthrough and remarkable gaming experiences.

AI has evolved from its humble beginnings to become a strong force that is constantly reshaping the game industry. As we move forward, artificial intelligence will continue to open up new possibilities and provide tremendous benefits to both players and developers.

Complementary creative processes for developers and AI:
AI can boost human creativity by giving developers new tools, techniques, and options. By merging human ingenuity with AI computational skills, gaming experiences can be elevated to new heights, breaking down barriers and stretching the bounds of what is possible.

Improved accessibility and inclusivity
Enabling more players to enjoy gaming

experiences:
By using AI to generate personalized and adaptable gaming experiences, developers may cater to a wide range of skill levels, interests, and skills. This creates a more inclusive gaming environment, allowing more players to experience the pleasures of interactive entertainment.

Adaptive AI systems for all participants.
AI can be utilized to create adaptive systems that cater to the unique demands of each user, allowing more people to enjoy gaming experiences. For example, AI-powered speech-to-text and text-to-speech conversion systems can assist hearing-impaired players in engaging with in-game dialogues, whilst AI-generated alternate control schemes can make games more accessible to players with motor impairments.

Enhanced game development and cost savings

Reducing Development Time and Resources:
AI may dramatically reduce the time and resources needed for game development by automating time-consuming operations like asset creation, environmental design, and character animation. This not only speeds up development but also decreases production costs, making it easier for smaller studios to make high-quality games.

AI-enabled tools for level design and game balance:

AI-powered design tools can help developers create complex, well-balanced levels more quickly. By automating key portions of the design process, such as level generation, object placement, and game balancing, creators can devote more time to innovation and creativity, ultimately boosting the game's overall quality.

Riot Games' control center: AI-powered real-time game data analysis.

Adaptable Difficulty and Customized Player Experience

Customizable, player-centric gaming experiences:

AI can be used to provide unique game experiences based on the player's playstyle, preferences, and activities. This makes for a more interesting and interactive gaming experience because the game can dynamically adapt to each player, providing tailored content and gameplay aspects depending on their specific interests and abilities.

AI algorithms that adapt games to individual player abilities:
AI-powered dynamic difficulty adjustment (DDA) systems monitor the player's performance and adapt the game's difficulty level in real-time, resulting in a continually interesting and demanding experience. DDA is used in games like "Resident Evil 4" (2005) and "Left 4 Dead" (2008) to create a personalized experience that keeps players engaged and delighted.

Unprecedented immersion and realism.

Realistic physics, environmental effects, and graphics:
AI-powered physics engines, such as NVIDIA PhysX and Havok, have enabled realistic physics simulation in video games. These engines use AI algorithms to determine the movements of objects, particle systems, and fluid dynamics, effectively simulating real-world physics and increasing players' immersion in the game environment.

AI-powered character behavior and interactions:
AI now allows non-player characters (NPCs) to express more realistic emotions, reactions, and behaviors. This gives the user a more immersive experience because they are no longer engaging with basic written characters, but with complex,

dynamic entities that respond and adapt to varied game scenarios.

Chapter 4

A Technological Symphony: AI and Gaming Platforms.

AI technology has knitted itself into the very fabric of gaming platforms, transforming how we experience and interact with the virtual worlds we so enjoy. Gaming platforms have advanced dramatically by leveraging AI's intrinsic abilities in learning, adapting, and changing, paving the way for an exciting new era of gaming. Let's look at how AI has improved gaming platforms and influenced the future of interactive entertainment.

AI-Powered Cloud Gaming Services

Cloud gaming has evolved as a game-changing tool, freeing us from the constraints of hardware and allowing us to play on almost any platform. AI plays an important role in improving the user experience of cloud gaming platforms. Google Stadia, which is now shut down, uses machine learning to predict user inputs, reducing latency and providing a more responsive gaming experience. Furthermore, AI-powered compression algorithms may automatically modify streaming quality in response to network constraints, ensuring a smooth and entertaining experience even when bandwidth varies. As cloud gaming becomes more popular, AI will play an important role in ensuring that players have the greatest experience possible.

By incorporating AI into gaming systems, developers have been able to push the bounds of visual and performance capabilities. This technical symphony has enabled increasingly immersive gaming experiences that engage our senses and spark our imaginations. As AI evolves, we may expect these developments to accelerate, resulting in even more breathtaking virtual worlds for us to explore and enjoy.

AI-Enhanced Graphics Processor
The quest for photorealism in gaming has long been a goal for developers, and AI has emerged as a valuable ally in accomplishing it. NVIDIA's Deep Learning Super Sampling (DLSS) technology is a prime example. DLSS uses AI algorithms to intelligently upscale lower-resolution photos, resulting in spectacular visuals while preserving peak performance. Similarly, ray tracing technology benefits from AI by more effectively producing realistic lighting and reflections through denoising algorithms. By merging AI with better graphics

processors, we may anticipate our games to have more lifelike graphics.

AI and Gaming Community

Gaming communities have expanded into massive social networks that rely on player contact, collaboration, and shared experiences. AI has stepped up to improve and support these communities by encouraging communication, facilitating teamwork, and maintaining a positive atmosphere. Let's look further into how artificial intelligence is transforming gaming communities and connecting people all around the world.

Creating and Supporting Gaming Communities

Creating a secure and inclusive atmosphere is critical for flourishing gaming communities. AI-powered technologies can monitor and manage communities by monitoring player behavior, sentiment, and engagement. By spotting and correcting disruptive behavior, AI can contribute to a more positive environment for all members. Furthermore, AI may be used to personalize material, adapting community updates and news to specific participants, ensuring that they are continually engaged and involved in their community.

As AI continues to integrate into gaming communities, we can expect more advanced tools and technologies to develop, further strengthening player bonds and providing a more pleasurable and engaging experience. AI and people will continue to collaborate because they share a passion for gaming, ensuring that gaming communities remain varied, lively, and supportive environments for gamers to connect, create, and thrive.

Fostering Communication and Collaboration
In an age where internet gaming connects millions of people from all over the world, good communication is more crucial than ever. AI-powered chatbots and virtual assistants can help players communicate more effectively by delivering real-time translations, assisting with in-game chores, and offering instruction as needed. AI-powered recommendation systems can also assess player behavior and interests, bringing together like-minded individuals and encouraging collaboration within gaming communities.

Chapter 5

AI in game development

In just a few years, AI may play a larger role in game development than in gameplay. Recent efforts with deep learning technology have enabled AI to learn from a sequence of images and text and repeat the experience.

Artificial intelligence is being used to generate pieces of art that resemble Picassos and emails that appear to have been authored by humans. The same technology is being utilized to create games.

In one experiment, artificial intelligence was able to program a level in a playable game using only images.

This technology is getting more dependable, and AI can quickly build a wide range of open-world games, which can then be tweaked by developers.

This will accelerate the development process. Deep fake technology and facial recognition software are also emerging, and they could play a significant part in future product development cycles.

Deep fake technology allows an AI to recognize and use different faces that it scans.

Although it is still in its infancy, this sort of AI can scan faces and generate stunningly accurate 3D models.

Consider how the same technology could be utilized to produce a structure or landscape. This would save developers numerous hours.

It is possible that an AI could employ all of these technologies to construct a fully functional game without the need for developers.

These AIs may be able to design games totally from scratch, guided by players' interests and habits.

This will enable them to develop personalized experiences for each gamer. Although it is difficult to estimate when this will happen, it is not surprising that AI will play a larger part in game creation in the next years.

What are the top five AI advances in the game industry?

AI and Procedural Generation

1. Endless Exploration and Discovery - Each level can reveal new places, secret treasures, unusual encounters, and so on, allowing for a more in-depth exploration of the game universe.

2. Dynamic and adaptive environments allow the game world to evolve, renew, and modify in response to player interactions and behavior.
3. Efficiency and Scalability: Create larger, more complex settings in less time.
4. Infinite Content Possibilities - Improves replayability and game longevity.

AI and NPCs

1. Collaborative NPCs - In multi-player gameplay, they might be cooperative teammates or opponents.
2. Dynamic Social Interactions - NPCs can express emotions, create relationships, and respond to the player's decisions and actions. Dynamic World Simulation - NPCs can participate in dynamic simulated activities such as trade and exploring.
3. Adaptive NPCs can change their behavior, methods, and responses over time.
4. Personalized Experiences - Custom quests, dialogue options, and prizes at the appropriate times will immerse players in the game.
5. Advanced AI behavior: NPCs can assess the game environment, interact with players, and make complicated decisions based on goals, emotions, and context.

AI and Game Balancing

1. Continuous Improvement - AI allows for continuing adjustment of game balance via game updates and patches.

2. Rapid Iteration and Testing - AI can simulate numerous test scenarios to detect imbalances, defects, and so forth.

3. Fair and competitive. Multi-player - Algorithms generate balanced matchups in multiplayer games.

4. Automated Balancing: Based on the player's performance, AI can dynamically modify

5. AI can learn from player behavior and preferences to improve game balance.

AI and Game Design.

1. Proactive Game Design entails creating game mechanics, challenges, and materials that meet the expectations of the players.

2. Player Behavior Analysis - Improves the overall game creation process.

3. Intelligent NPCs - Improve storytelling, develop memorable characters, and bring the gaming world to life.

4. Procedural Generation – Reduces the amount of manual work necessary for content production.

AI and Gaming Analytics

1. Fraud Detection & Security - Analyze data trends to identify and prevent fraudulent activity.

2. Predictive Analytics enables developers to anticipate player requirements and attrition rates, optimizing game content and features accordingly.

3. Adaptive Gameplay - AI can adapt to difficult stages, tempo, and content. Live Operations and Updates - Game developers can evaluate game performance, user feedback, emotion, and so on.

4. Player Insights - Make data-driven decisions to improve game design and revenue strategies.

Chapter 6

What is the future of AI in the gaming industry?

The use of AI in game design and development has advanced significantly, and it shows no indications of slowing. Let us examine what the future seems to store.

- ❖ **Improved Mobile Gaming Experience.**
  Mobile gaming is a growing trend that allows players to access an infinite number of games from wherever they are. Phone manufacturers have focused on building devices that can handle high-resolution and graphically intensive content.

- ❖ **Wearables Support Gaming and VR Gaming.**
  The evolution of AR, VR, and MR has raised the bar for experiencing games based on virtual and mixed reality, making them more realistic and advanced in terms of entertainment. The Oculus Quest is an all-in-one PC-quality virtual reality device and the best example of a wearable gadget for wearable gaming.

❖ **Blockchain-Based Gaming**
Blockchain-based gaming is currently a relatively unknown topic. To play these games, gamers and creators must collaborate on the blockchain network. At the same time, to participate in this game community, users must own or own digital properties.

❖ **Cloud-based gaming using AI.**
Cloud gaming is a technology that allows users to stream games over the Internet rather than downloading and installing them. This technology has been in development for several years, but it has yet to become widely adopted.

❖ **Voice or Audio Recognition-Based Games**
The use of audio recognition in gaming will alter our perception of the medium. Voice recognition in gaming allows the user to manage game movements, monitor controls, and even eliminate the need for a controller.

Business Impacts of AI in the Gaming Industry
As AI continues to have a substantial impact on numerous elements of the gaming industry, it is also changing the way games are funded, marketed, and managed. AI is altering the industry by paving the way for new income models and improving marketing techniques, as well as creating new prospects for expansion. Let's look at how artificial intelligence is changing the gaming business.

Influencing Marketing Strategies
AI's ability to process and analyze large volumes of data on player behavior, demographics, and preferences is extremely beneficial to gaming companies looking to improve their marketing efforts. Businesses may use AI-driven analytics to build more focused and effective advertising campaigns, identifying which channels and messages resonate with their target demographic. Furthermore, AI may assist in identifying trends and patterns in player involvement, allowing businesses to optimize their marketing resources and efforts to maximize user acquisition, retention, and lifetime value.

Marketing Strategy	AI Technology	Impact on Gaming
Dynamic pricing	AI-driven price optimization	Customized pricing techniques to boost revenue and user retention
Personalized recommendations.	Content-based or collaborative filtering	Increasing user pleasure and engagement through personalized game ideas
User Segmentation	Machine learning.	Identifying key players and maximizing marketing resources
Targeted advertising	AI-powered analytics	Enhanced ad relevancy, improving user engagement, and click-through rates.

New revenue models.
AI's ability to assess and comprehend individual player preferences and behavior creates prospects for new business models in the gaming industry. For example, AI-powered dynamic pricing tactics can be used to provide personalized in-game items, promotions, or adverts to each player. This personalized strategy benefits both players and developers because it boosts player engagement and revenue through customized offers. Furthermore, AI-powered recommendation systems can be used for subscription-based gaming services, increasing customer happiness by providing games that are suited to their preferences.

Companies in the gaming sector can use AI to provide more personalized experiences, make income through tailored offers, and enhance marketing efforts to better reach their customers. As AI technology advances and is more deeply integrated into gaming, its impact on the business side of the industry will grow, ushering in a new era of creativity and financial success.

AI for E-Sports and Competitive Gaming
The world of e-sports and competitive gaming has expanded rapidly in recent years, and artificial intelligence has played a critical part in defining this thrilling environment. Let's look at the different

ways AI has influenced e-sports and competitive gaming:

Making the Call: AI-Assisted Refereeing and Fair Play.

Artificial intelligence can help ensure fair play in e-sports by identifying cheating and supporting referees with decision-making. Using AI, event organizers can evaluate in-game behaviors to identify potential incidents of hacking, scripting, or other forms of cheating, ensuring that e-sports tournaments are fair and entertaining for all players. Riot Games, the creators of "League of Legends," launched an AI technology called "Intentional Feeder Detection" to identify and penalize players who purposefully undermine their team's prospects of victory.

Analyzing the Game: AI-Powered Analytics and Strategies

AI-powered analytics systems can provide useful insights into gameplay data, allowing teams and players to make better judgments regarding their strategies and tactics. By analyzing vast amounts of data, AI can detect patterns, trends, and insights that human analysts might miss, providing competitive players an advantage in the e-sports field. Companies such as Mobalytics and Shadow.gg provide AI-powered analytics tools for games such as "League of Legends" and "Counter-Strike: Global Offensive," giving players and coaches a lot of information to help them better their skills.

A New Type of Competition: AI Competitors in E-Sports Tournaments

AI can completely transform e-sports by establishing a new class of non-human rivals. For example, the annual StarCraft AI competition shows the abilities of AI-powered players, challenging human players with distinct tactics and techniques that evolve.

AI for E-Sports and Competitive Gaming	Description	Impact on the E-Sports Industry.
AI-assisted Anti-cheating Systems	Artificial intelligence systems detect and prevent cheating in online competitive gaming situations.	Fair and safe gaming experiences, preserving the integrity of e-sports tournaments.
AI Game Spectator Enhancements	AI algorithms provide real-time insights, analytics, and enhancements for live game	Improved viewer experience, enhancing engagement and audience

	broadcasts.	retention.
AI-powered coaching tools.	AI tools assess player strengths and weaknesses and provide individualized coaching and training recommendations.	Improved player performance and skill growth, resulting in more competitive gaming
AI-driven Analytics	AI programs evaluate player performance, game trends, and strategy.	Improved decision-making in team management, player training, and game plan creation.

Test the Best: AI as a Training Tool for Professional Players.

AI-powered opponents have become a useful resource for professional gamers, supplying them with difficult foes who can adapt and learn from the user's play style. By practicing against AI opponents, gamers can improve their skills, detect potential flaws, and devise new techniques.
A well-known example of AI in this area is OpenAI's "Dota 2" bot, which defeated professional gamers in 1v1 matches at The International 201

Conclusion

AI is driving the advancement of video games, allowing for more immersive, intelligent, and dynamic gameplay experiences. AI-powered features and characters improve immersion, challenge players, and push the frontiers of interactive entertainment by utilizing complex algorithms, machine-learning approaches, and imaginative design.

www.ingramcontent.com/pod-product-compliance
Lightning Source LLC
Chambersburg PA
CBHW070949220526
45471CB00007B/2950